i ♥ love my
soup
maker

 CookNation

I LOVE MY SOUP MAKER
THE ONLY SOUP MACHINE RECIPE BOOK YOU'LL EVER NEED

ISBN 978-1-911219-18-7

DISCLAIMER

This book is designed to provide information on soups that can be made using electric soup maker appliances, results may differ if alternative devices are used.

Some recipes may contain nuts or traces of nuts. Those suffering from any allergies associated with nuts should avoid any recipes containing nuts or nut based oils.
This information is provided and sold with the knowledge that the publisher and author do not offer any legal or other professional advice. In the case of a need for any such expertise consult with the appropriate professional.
This book does not contain all information available on the subject, and other sources of recipes are available.
Every effort has been made to make this book as accurate as possible. However, there may be typographical and or content errors. Therefore, this book should serve only as a general guide and not as the ultimate source of subject information.
This book contains information that might be dated and is intended only to educate and entertain.
The author and publisher shall have no liability or responsibility to any person or entity regarding any loss or damage incurred, or alleged to have incurred, directly or indirectly, by the information contained in this book.

CONTENTS

MEAT AND POULTRY SOUPS

FISH AND SEAFOOD SOUPS 73

SOUPS AROUND THE WORLD 89

OTHER COOK NATION TITLES 101

You may also enjoy.....

LOW CALORIE, HEALTHY AND SIMPLE SOUP MACHINE RECIPES UNDER 100, 200 AND 300 CALORIES. PERFECT FOR ANY DIET AND WEIGHT LOSS PLAN.

ISBN 978-1-909855-02-1

SIMPLE, HEALTHY & DELICIOUS LOW CALORIE SOUP RECIPES FOR YOUR SLOW COOKER. ALL UNDER 100, 200 & 300 CALORIES.

ISBN 978-1-909855-30-4

INTRODUCTION

I love my soup maker is a recipe book celebrating the wonderful world of soup.

Versatile, diverse, healthy, with a multitude of different flavours and inspirations from around the world soup is the perfect meal, side dish or snack all year round.

With your electric soup maker soup is incredibly easy to prepare. It's economical, makes use of whatever leftovers you have in the kitchen and can be made ahead to be frozen and used later. Ranging from the very simplest soups to exotic recipes you will find inspiration here.

The recipes in this book are all written for use with an electric soup maker but can also be used if you prefer the more traditional stove-top method of soup making.

SOUP IS JUST FOR COLD WINTER NIGHTS, RIGHT?

Wrong! While there is nothing better than a bowl of comforting steaming hot broth on a miserable winter's day, soup isn't just for dark cold nights. It can be a vibrant and refreshing alternative on the brightest and hottest of days , and make use of the best seasonal ingredients all year round. Did you know that some soups can also be served chilled? What could be better on a summer's day?

WHAT MAKES A GREAT SOUP?

Thankfully you don't have to be a great chef to make an incredible soup and using a soup maker just makes everything even easier. There are however a few key elements to making a great soup.

The Base: the start to most soups requires a few vegetables to give your soup a rounded flavour. Onions, carrots and celery are a great start.

Stock: A good quality stock will make the world of difference to the quality of your soup. Use either vegetable, fish or meat stock and if you can make these at home, all the better. If you opt for store-bought stock try to choose a good quality product that is not high in sodium.

Ingredients: Soup is so versatile that almost any ingredient can be used whether you are looking for a meaty protein packed dish, an Asian seafood soup, or a thick vegetarian broth using beans and pulses. Certain ingredients will change the consistency of your soup too, for example potatoes and lentils will thicken, while adding some single cream will make it smoother.

Seasoning: Most soups will require some seasoning. Be careful when choosing your stock that it is not overly high in its sodium content. There are also many popular herbs that compliment soups such as marjoram, thyme, parsley, sage, rosemary, oregano and of course salt and pepper. You should also feel free to experiment. For example: Garlic, ginger and coriander can work well in Asian soups while cumin, turmeric or garam masala can give an authentic Indian feel to your dish.

Garnish: There is nothing better than serving a homemade soup with a little garnish, which not only looks the part but also adds an extra taste. Depending on your dish, freshly chopped herbs, croutons, a little cream, crème fraiche or freshly grated parmesan are all great finishing touches.

WHICH SOUP MAKER?

If you are reading this you will no doubt already have purchased a soup maker. For those who have not, or are considering replacing their appliance there are a few basic considerations when purchasing a soup maker.

Model: There are 2 main styles of soup maker on the market at the moment. One resembles a traditional blender in appearance and the other a jug-style which looks a little like a modern kettle. The blender style is generally more expensive but offers more flexibility enabling you to brown-off base ingredients for example as well as adjust cooking times. This style also allows you to use the unit as a traditional blender for crushing ice, making smoothies etc. The glass jar also allows you to see the contents as they cook.

The jug/kettle style differs to the blender style by having the blades and motor in the lid of the appliance rather than the base. These units do not have a glass jar so you cannot see the contents while cooking therefore it is necessary to check fill levels to avoid over-filling. There is no option to brown ingredients with this type of machine. This type of soup maker is very easy to use with pre-programmed settings.

Size: Soup makers have different capacities depending on the quantity of soup you need to make. They generally range from 1.0 to 1.7 litres. Make your choice of capacity dependant on your needs but remember that you can freeze soup so any extras can be used for another meal.

Power: This will determine how powerful the appliance will chop and blend. Generally a more powerful motor may see better results but not always! Also a more powerful machine may heat up your soup quicker.

Settings: There should be multiple heating settings. Usually low, medium, high and simmer. Depending which model you have (blender style or jug/kettle style) you will also have a timer or pre-programmed settings.

Non-stick Heating Plate: Most appliances will advertise this as a feature. You will no doubt know from your own experience that ingredients can sometimes stick and can be stubborn to remove afterwards. Make sure you carefully read reviews of the product before purchasing and follow manufacturer's guidelines for use.

Stir Function: This is a handy addition which allows the soup to be stirred by the appliance at regular intervals and can prevent sticking.

Cleaning: Whilst using a soup maker certainly reduces the washing up, the unit itself does still need to be cleaned afterwards. Some appliances are easier to clean than others. Research how easily blades and elements of the unit can be removed for cleaning and again pay attention to reviews of those who have already purchased.

TIPS FOR USING YOUR SOUP MAKER

- Prepare all your ingredients first.
- Use hot stock in recipes, not cold.
- Cut your ingredients into small bite size pieces before adding to the soup maker.
- To prevent sticking use a little oil when sautéing.
- Do not use frozen ingredients as this will increase cooking times.
- Allow any frozen ingredients to thaw first.
- Do not use any meat with bones in the soup maker
- Do not use any seafood which are still in their shells in the soup maker
- Do not use raw meat or seafood – only cooked.
- If fitted, use the stir function regularly.
- Always make sure the lid is tightly closed and fastened before cooking.
- Follow the manufacturer's safety guidelines when using the appliance, particularly when opening the lid after or during cooking, which may release scalding steam.
- Do not overfill your appliance. Pay careful attention to the capacity of your machine and the fill level markers. There are different levels for cold and hot liquids.
- Be careful of fully immersing your jug in water as this may result in short-circuiting the machine.
- Allow the soup maker to fully cool before attempting to clean. Heating plates and blades may still be very hot.
- Most soup makers are not dishwasher safe so must be cleaned manually. Warm soapy water should be sufficient. If the heating plate has become burned, soak in hot soapy water for longer and use a coarse sponge to remove. Avoid using any harsh cleaning products or scouring pads, as these will damage the surface of the heating plate.
- Read the manufactures instructions and guidelines for your appliance thoroughly before using. These will provide information, tips and safety guidelines specific to your product and should be adhered to in order to get the best out of your appliance.

ALL RECIPES ARE A GUIDE ONLY

All the recipes in this book are a guide only which have been created for use in a large family sized soup maker. You may need to alter quantities and cooking times to suit your own appliance – do not overfill your soup maker.

Consistency is also a question of personal preference. Some recipes suggest the best consistency to use; others leave it to your own personal taste. Feel free to experiment by adding more or less liquid to suit your own taste.

ABOUT COOKNATION

CookNation is the leading publisher of innovative and practical recipe books for the modern, health conscious cook.

CookNation titles bring together delicious, easy and practical recipes with their unique approach - easy and delicious, no-nonsense recipes - making cooking for diets and healthy eating fast, simple and fun.

With a range of #1 best-selling titles - from the innovative 'Skinny' calorie-counted series, to the 5:2 Diet Recipes collection - CookNation recipe books prove that 'Diet' can still mean 'Delicious'!

 **CookNation**

Homemade Stock

Homemade stock is not essential for any soup making, but if you fancy having a go you will find it can add additional depth of taste and further improve the flavour of some dishes. Having said that, shop bought stock has vastly improved in recent times and you may well decide making your own stock isn't worth the time for the comparable result. If you do use shop bought stock (which most people do) avoid buying budget options and anything too high in sodium.

Use a large pan rather than your soup maker as you will want to make bigger quantities.

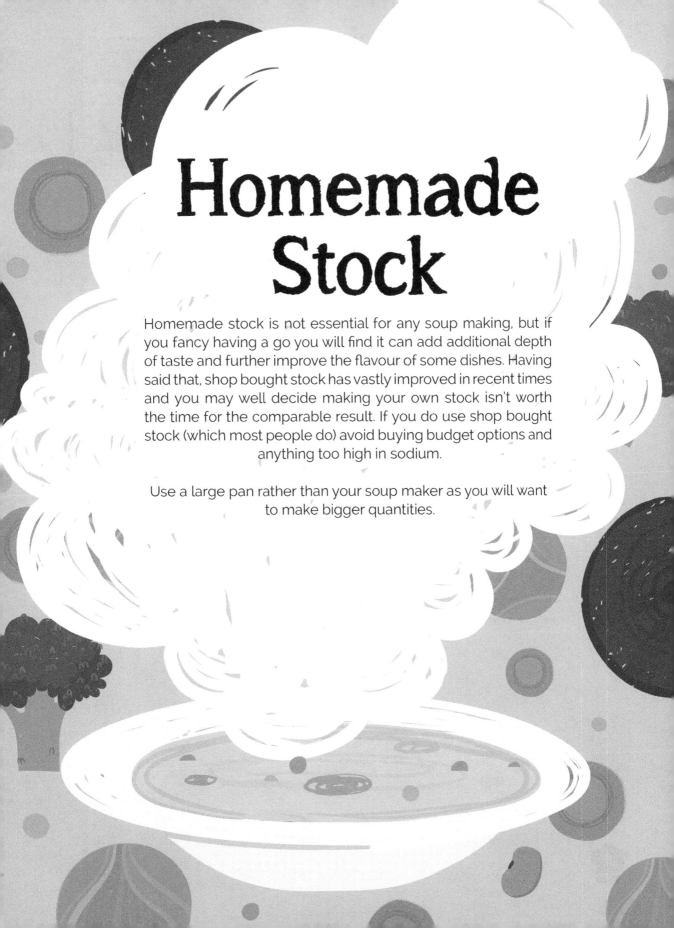

BASIC VEGETABLE STOCK

Ingredients

- 1 tbsp olive oil
- 1 onion, chopped
- 1 leek, chopped
- 1 carrot, chopped
- 1 small bulb fennel, chopped
- 3 garlic cloves, crushed
- 1 tbsp black peppercorns

- 75g/3oz mushrooms
- 2 sticks celery, chopped
- 3 tomatoes, diced
- 2 tbsp freshly chopped flat leaf parsley
- 2 bay leaves
- 3lt/12 cups water

Method

Gently sauté the onions, leeks, carrots and fennel in the olive oil for a few minutes in a large lidded saucepan. Add all the other ingredients, cover and bring to the boil. Leave to gently simmer for 20 minutes with the lid on. Allow to cool for a little while. Pour the contents through a sieve and store the finished stock liquid in the fridge for a couple of days or freeze in batches.

BASIC CHICKEN STOCK

Ingredients

- 1 tbsp olive oil
- 1 left over roast chicken carcass
- 2 carrots, chopped
- 2 onions, halved
- 2 stalks celery, chopped

- 10 black peppercorns
- 2 bay leaves
- 2 tbsp freshly chopped parsley
- 1 tsp freshly chopped thyme
- 3lt/12 cups water

Method

Gently sauté the onions, carrots and celery in the olive oil for a few minutes in a large lidded saucepan. Break the chicken carcass up into pieces and add to the pan along with all the other ingredients, cover and bring to the boil. Leave to very gently simmer for 1hr with the lid on. Allow to cool for a little while. Pour the contents through a sieve and store the finished stock liquid in the fridge for a couple of days or freeze in batches. You may find you need to skim a little fat from the top of the stock after cooking.

BASIC FISH STOCK

Ingredients

- 1 tbsp olive oil
- 450g/1lb fish bones, heads carcasses etc (avoid oily fish when making stock)
- 4 leeks, chopped
- 1 fennel bulb, chopped
- 4 carrots, chopped
- 2 tbsp freshly chopped parsley
- 250ml/1 cup dry white wine
- 2.5lt/10 cups water

Method

Gently sauté the carrots, leeks and fennel in the olive oil for a few minutes in a large lidded saucepan. Clean the fish bones to ensure there is no blood as this can 'spoil' the stock. Add all the other ingredients, cover and bring to the boil. Leave to very gently simmer for 1hr with the lid on. Allow to cool for a little while. Pour the contents through a sieve and store the finished stock liquid in the fridge for a couple of days or freeze in batches. You may find you need to skim a little fat from the top of the stock after cooking.

ASPARAGUS AND SPRING ONION SOUP

Ingredients

- 1 tbsp olive oil
- 6 spring onions/scallions, chopped
- 1 medium onion, peeled and chopped
- 250g/9oz asparagus, chopped
- 1 medium potato, peeled and chopped
- 1lt/4 cups vegetable stock/broth
- Salt and pepper to taste

Method

1 Choose your preferred blend function, if required – smooth is recommended for this soup. Otherwise decide on your consistency at the end of cooking and then blend.

2 If your soup maker has a browning function, add the olive oil, onions and spring onions first, and leave to brown for a few minutes.

3 Add all the ingredients to the soup maker and mix well. Cover and leave to cook on high for around 30 minutes. Ensure all the ingredients are well combined, tender and piping hot. Blend on the smooth setting. Adjust the seasoning and serve.

CHEFS NOTE
This makes a lovely thick soup, stir in a little cream when you serve.

CARROT AND GINGER SOUP

Ingredients

- 1 tbsp olive oil
- 1 large onion, peeled and chopped
- 1 tsp fresh grated ginger
- 4 medium carrots, peeled and chopped

- 1 tsp salt
- 1lt/4 cups vegetable stock/broth
- Coloured peppercorns, ground, to garnish (optional)

Method

1 Choose your preferred blend function, if required. Otherwise decide on your consistency at the end of cooking and then blend.

2 If your soup maker has a browning function, add the olive oil, onions and ginger first and leave to brown for a few minutes.

3 Add all the ingredients, except the peppercorns, to the soup maker. Cover and leave to cook on high for 40 minutes. Ensure all the ingredients are well combined, tender and piping hot. Blend to your preferred consistency (or leave your machine to do this as programmed). Serve garnished with the ground peppercorns.

CHEFS NOTE

If your soup maker doesn't have a browning function, frying the onions and ginger in a pan before adding them to the soup maker will bring out a stronger flavour.

TRADITIONAL VEGETABLE SOUP

Ingredients

- 1 tbsp olive oil
- 1 medium onion, peeled and chopped
- 2 medium potatoes, peeled and chopped
- 2 medium carrots, peeled and chopped
- ½ medium red bell pepper, de-seeded chopped
- 1 clove garlic, crushed

- 1 stalk celery, chopped
- ½ medium swede, peeled and chopped
- 75g/3oz green beans
- 1lt/4 cups vegetable stock/broth
- 1 tsp dried oregano
- Salt and pepper to taste

Method

1 Choose your preferred blend function, if required. Otherwise decide on your consistency at the end of cooking and then blend.

2 If your soup maker has a browning function, add the olive oil and onions first and leave to brown for a few minutes.

3 Add all the ingredients to the soup maker. Cover and leave to cook on high for 40 minutes. Ensure all the ingredients are well combined, tender and piping hot. Blend to your preferred consistency (or leave your machine to do this as programmed). Stir in the oregano and cook for a further 3 or 4 minutes. Adjust the seasoning and serve.

CHEFS NOTE
Feel free to use whichever vegetables you have to hand.

PEA AND LETTUCE SOUP

Ingredients

- Knob of butter
- 2 medium leeks, sliced
- 750ml/3 cups vegetable stock/broth
- 2 medium potatoes, peeled and chopped
- 200g/7oz sugar snap peas, trimmed

- 2 romaine hearts, chopped
- 3 tbsp fresh tarragon
- 250ml/1 cup single cream
- Salt and pepper to taste

Method

1 Choose your preferred blend function, if required. Otherwise decide on your consistency at the end of cooking and then blend.

2 If your soup maker has a browning function, add the butter and leeks first and leave to brown for a few minutes.

3 Add all the ingredients, except the chopped romaine, tarragon and cream, to the soup maker. Cover and leave to cook on high for 30 minutes. Add the chopped romaine and tarragon, stir and leave to cook for a further 5 minutes. Ensure all the ingredients are well combined, tender and piping hot.

4 Blend to your preferred consistency (or leave your machine to do this as programmed). Stir in the cream. Adjust the seasoning and serve.

CHEFS NOTE

You can use ordinary milk instead of cream if you prefer.

PUMPKIN SOUP

Ingredients

- 1 tbsp olive oil
- 1 large onion, peeled and chopped
- 400g/14oz pumpkin, peeled and chopped
- 1 medium carrot, peeled and chopped
- 1 medium potato, peeled and chopped
- Salt & pepper
- 1lt/4 cups vegetable stock/broth

Method

1 Choose your preferred blend function, if required. Otherwise decide on your consistency at the end of cooking and then blend.

2 If your soup maker has a browning function, add the olive oil and onions first and leave to brown for a few minutes.

3 Add all the ingredients to the soup maker. Cover and leave to cook on high for 40 minutes. Ensure all the ingredients are well combined, tender and piping hot. Blend to your preferred consistency (or leave your machine to do this as programmed).

4 Adjust the seasoning and serve.

CHEFS NOTE
Garnish with a swirl of cream and a sprig of parsley.

TOMATO AND RED PEPPER SOUP

Ingredients

- Knob of butter
- 1 medium onion, peeled and chopped
- 1 clove garlic, crushed
- 2 medium red bell peppers, de-seeded and chopped
- 1½ tbsp tomato puree/paste
- 1 tsp smoked paprika

- 1 400g/14oz tin peeled plum tomatoes with basil
- 750ml/3 cups vegetable stock/broth
- ½ tsp brown sugar
- Salt and pepper to taste
- 60ml/¼ cup double cream
- 1 tbsp chopped fresh basil

Method

1 Choose your preferred blend function, if required. Otherwise decide on your consistency at the end of cooking and then blend.

2 If your soup maker has a browning function, add the olive oil, onions and garlic first and leave to brown for a few minutes.

3 Add all the ingredients, except the basil and cream, to the soup maker. Cover and leave to cook on high for 30 minutes. Ensure all the ingredients are well combined, tender and piping hot. Blend to your preferred consistency (or leave your machine to do this as programmed). Stir in the basil and cream. Adjust the seasoning and serve.

CHEFS NOTE
Try served with cheese croutons and chopped chives.

CREAM OF LEEK AND POTATO SOUP

Ingredients

- 1 tbsp olive oil
- 2 medium leeks, chopped
- 1 medium onion, peeled and chopped
- 2 medium potatoes, peeled and chopped
- 1lt/4 cups vegetable stock/broth
- Salt and pepper
- 120ml/½ cup fresh cream

Method

1 Choose your preferred blend function (smooth is recommended for this recipe) if required. Otherwise decide on your consistency at the end of cooking and then blend.

2 If your soup maker has a browning function, add the olive oil, leeks and onions first and leave to brown for a couple of minutes.

3 Add all the ingredients, except the cream, to the soup maker. Cover and leave to cook on high for about 20 minutes. Ensure all the ingredients are well combined, tender and piping hot. Blend on the smooth setting (or leave your machine to do this as programmed). Stir in the cream. Adjust the seasoning and serve.

CHEFS NOTE
Serve garnished with parsley, and lots of fresh, crusty bread.

BROCCOLI BISQUE

Ingredients

- Knob of butter
- ½ medium onion, peeled and chopped
- Handful baby spinach
- 750ml/3 cups vegetable stock/broth

- 675g/1½ lb broccoli florets
- 120ml/½ cup double cream
- Greek yogurt to garnish (optional)
- Lemon zest to garnish (optional)

Method

1 Choose your preferred blend function, if required - smooth is recommended for this recipe. Otherwise decide on your consistency at the end of cooking and then blend.

2 If your soup maker has a browning function, add the butter and onions first and leave to brown for a few minutes.

3 Add all the ingredients, apart from the cream, yogurt and lemon zest, to the soup maker. Cover and leave to cook on high for around 20 minutes. Ensure all the ingredients are well combined, tender and piping hot. Blend on the smooth setting (or leave your machine to do this as programmed).

4 Stir in the cream. Adjust the seasoning and serve with a spoonful of Greek yogurt and a sprinkling of lemon zest.

CHEFS NOTE
Add additional stock for a thinner consistency.

CREAM OF TOMATO SOUP

Ingredients

- 1lt/4 cups tomato passata/sieved tomatoes
- 2 tsp brown sugar
- 1 400g/14oz tin plum tomatoes

- 2 vegetable stock cubes, crumbled
- 2 tbsp tomato puree/paste
- 120ml/½ cup whole milk
- Salt & pepper to taste

Method

1 Choose your preferred blend function, if required. Smooth is recommended for this recipe. Otherwise decide on your consistency at the end of cooking and then blend.

2 Add all the ingredients to the soup maker. Cover and leave to cook on high for 30 minutes. Ensure all the ingredients are well combined, tender and piping hot. Blend on the smooth setting (or leave your machine to do this as programmed). Adjust the seasoning and serve.

CHEFS NOTE

If you plan to freeze this soup, you may wish to leave out the milk and add it in when you're ready to reheat and eat.

MUSHROOM SQUASH SOUP

Ingredients

- Knob of butter
- 1 large onion, peeled and chopped
- 300g/11oz mushrooms, sliced
- 2 medium carrots, peeled and chopped
- 1 stalk celery, chopped
- ½ butternut squash, peeled and chopped
- 750ml/3 cups vegetable stock/broth
- 1 tsp salt
- 1 tbsp fresh lemon juice

Method

1 Choose your preferred blend function, if required. Otherwise decide on your consistency at the end of cooking and then blend.

2 If your soup maker has a browning function, add the butter, onions and mushrooms first and leave to brown for a few minutes.

3 Add all the ingredients except the lemon juice to the soup maker. Cover and leave to cook on high for 40 minutes. Ensure all the ingredients are well combined, tender and piping hot. Blend to your preferred consistency (or leave your machine to do this as programmed). Stir in the lemon juice. Adjust the seasoning and serve.

CHEFS NOTE
Experiment with types and mixtures of mushrooms for subtle differences in flavour.

WINTER VEGETABLE AND LENTIL SOUP

Ingredients

- 1 medium potato, peeled and chopped
- 2 large carrots, peeled and chopped
- 1 medium swede, peeled and chopped.
- 50g/2oz lentils, rinsed and drained

- 1 clove garlic, crushed
- ½ tsp ground cinnamon
- 1l4/4 cups vegetable stock/broth
- Salt and pepper

Method

1 Choose your preferred blend function, if required. Otherwise decide on your consistency at the end of cooking and then blend.

2 Add all the ingredients to the soup maker. Cover and leave to cook on high for 40 minutes. Ensure all the ingredients are well combined, tender and piping hot. Blend to your preferred consistency (or leave your machine to do this as programmed). Adjust the seasoning and serve.

CHEFS NOTE

Feel free to change around your winter vegetables, e.g. use parsnips, sweet potatoes etc.

APPLE AND BEETROOT SOUP

Ingredients

- 1 tbsp olive oil
- 1 small onion, peeled and chopped
- 450g/1lb beetroot, cooked, peeled and chopped
- 2 green apples, cored, peeled, sliced
- Salt and pepper
- 1lt/4 cups vegetable stock/broth

Method

1 Choose your preferred blend function – smooth is recommended for this recipe - if required. Otherwise decide on your consistency at the end of cooking and then blend.

2 If your soup maker has a browning function, add the olive oil and onions first and leave to brown for a few minutes.

3 Add all the ingredients to the soup maker. Cover and leave to cook on high for 40 minutes. Ensure all the ingredients are well combined, tender and piping hot. Blend on the smooth setting (or leave your machine to do this as programmed). Adjust the seasoning and serve.

CHEFS NOTE
Delicious served with a spoonful of soured cream.

ORANGE AND BEETROOT SOUP

Ingredients

- 1 tbsp olive oil
- 1 large red onion, peeled and chopped
- 550g/1¼ lb beetroots, cooked, peeled and chopped

- 2 medium carrots, peeled and chopped
- 750ml/3 cups vegetable stock/broth
- 250ml/1 cup fresh orange juice
- Salt and pepper

Method

1 Choose your preferred blend function, if required - the smooth setting is recommended for this recipe. Otherwise decide on your consistency at the end of cooking and then blend.

2 If your soup maker has a browning function, add the olive oil and onions first and leave to brown for a few minutes.

3 Add all the ingredients, except the orange juice, to the soup maker. Cover and leave to cook on high for 40 minutes. Ensure all the ingredients are well combined, tender and piping hot. Blend on the smooth setting (or leave your machine to do this as programmed). Stir in the orange juice and leave to warm through for a further minute. Adjust the seasoning and serve.

CHEFS NOTE
Try using apple juice rather than fresh orange juice.

FRENCH SPRING ONION SOUP

Ingredients

- Large knob of unsalted butter
- 1 tbsp olive oil
- 10 spring onions/scallions, chopped
- 1 medium onion, peeled and chopped
- 2 tbsp sherry
- 750ml/3 cups vegetable stock/broth
- 1 tbsp lemon juice
- Salt and pepper
- Gruyère cheese, grated, to garnish

Method

1 Choose your preferred blend function, if required. Otherwise decide on your consistency at the end of cooking and then blend.

2 If your soup maker has a browning function, add the olive oil, half the butter, the spring onions and onions first, and leave to brown for a few minutes.

3 Add all the ingredients to the soup maker except the cheese and remaining butter.. Cover and leave to cook on high for 30 minutes. Ensure all the ingredients are well combined, tender and piping hot. Blend to your preferred consistency (or leave your machine to do this as programmed). Stir in the rest of the butter. Adjust the seasoning and serve garnished with the grated cheese.

CHEFS NOTE

Unless you're serving this soup to vegetarians, consider also trying it with a rich beef stock/broth.

CAULIFLOWER AND BROCCOLI SOUP

Ingredients

- 2 medium carrots, peeled and chopped
- ¼ large cauliflower, chopped
- 1 head broccoli, chopped
- Salt and pepper
- 1lt/4 cups vegetable stock/broth

Method

1 Choose your preferred blend function, if required – the smooth setting is recommended for this recipe. Otherwise decide on your consistency at the end of cooking and then blend.

2 Add all the ingredients to the soup maker. Cover and leave to cook on high for 30 minutes. Ensure all the ingredients are well combined, tender and piping hot. Blend on the smooth setting (or leave your machine to do this as programmed). Season and serve.

CHEFS NOTE
This simple soup is delicious with any mixture of vegetables you have to hand.

RED LENTIL, TOMATO AND SPINACH SOUP

Ingredients

- 1 tbsp olive oil
- 1 medium onion, peeled and chopped
- 4 medium carrots, peeled and chopped
- 1 400g/14oz tin chopped tomatoes

- 750ml/3 cups vegetable stock/broth
- 200g/7oz dried red lentils, rinsed
- Salt and pepper
- Handful baby spinach

Method

1 Choose your preferred blend function, if required. Otherwise decide on your consistency at the end of cooking and then blend.

2 If your soup maker has a browning function, add the olive oil, onions and carrots first and leave to brown for a few minutes.

3 Add all the ingredients, except the spinach, to the soup maker. Cover and leave to cook on high for 40 minutes. Ensure all the ingredients are well combined, tender and piping hot. Add the spinach and cook for another five minutes or so. Blend to your preferred consistency (or leave your machine to do this as programmed). Adjust the seasoning and serve.

CHEFS NOTE
Add more stock if needed to get the consistency right.

MUSHROOM AND PEPPERCORN SOUP

Ingredients

- 1 tbsp olive oil
- 1 medium onion, peeled and chopped
- 1 medium leek, chopped
- 400g/14oz mushrooms, finely chopped
- 1 tsp peppercorns, ground
- 1lt/4 cups vegetable stock/broth
- Chives, chopped, to garnish
- Double cream to garnish

Method

1 Choose your preferred blend function if required – smooth is recommended for this soup. Otherwise decide on your consistency at the end of cooking and then blend.

2 If your soup maker has a browning function, add the olive oil, onions and leeks first and leave to brown for a few minutes.

3 Add all the ingredients to the soup maker except the chopped chives and cream. Cover and leave to cook on high for 40 minutes. Ensure all the ingredients are well combined, tender and piping hot. Blend on the smooth setting (or leave your machine to do this as programmed). Adjust the seasoning and serve with a scattering of chopped chives and a spoonful of cream.

CHEFS NOTE

Adjust the peppercorn quantity to suit your own taste.

LENTIL AND SWEET POTATO SOUP

Ingredients

- 2 tbsp olive oil
- 1 large onion, peeled and chopped
- 2 garlic cloves, crushed
- 2 tsp mild curry powder
- 4 medium sweet potatoes, peeled and chopped
- 1 apple, peeled, cored and chopped
- 750ml/3 cups vegetable stock/broth
- 75g/3oz red lentils
- 250ml/1 cup milk
- 1 tbsp lime juice

Method

1 Choose your preferred blend function, if required. Otherwise decide on your consistency at the end of cooking and then blend.

2 If your soup maker has a browning function, add the olive oil, onions and garlic first and leave to brown for a few minutes.

3 Add all the ingredients, except the lime juice, to the soup maker. Cover and leave to cook on high for 40 minutes. Ensure all the ingredients are well combined, tender and piping hot. Blend to your preferred consistency (or leave your machine to do this as programmed). Stir in the lime juice. Adjust the seasoning and serve.

CHEFS NOTE
Garnish with some freshly chopped corriander/cilantro.

AUBERGINE AND BUTTER BEAN SOUP

Ingredients

- 1 medium aubergine/eggplant, cubed
- 200g/7oz butter beans
- 750ml/3 cups vegetable stock/broth
- 120ml/½ cup cream
- Salt and pepper to taste

Method

1 Choose your preferred blend function, if required. Otherwise decide on your consistency at the end of cooking and then blend.

2 Add all the ingredients, except the cream, to the soup maker. Cover and leave to cook on high for 30 minutes. Ensure all the ingredients are well combined, tender and piping hot. Blend to your preferred consistency (or leave your machine to do this as programmed). Stir in the cream and warm for a further minute. Adjust the seasoning and serve.

CHEFS NOTE
Delicious garnished with fresh basil or oregano.

SPICY VEGETABLE SOUP

Ingredients

- 2 tbsp olive oil
- 2 medium onions, peeled and chopped
- 2 medium sweet potatoes, peeled and chopped
- 2 medium carrots, peeled and chopped
- 2 medium parsnips, peeled and chopped

- 2 tsp medium curry powder
- 75g/3oz dried green lentils
- 750ml/3 cups vegetable stock/broth
- 250ml/1 cup milk
- Salt and pepper
- Greek yogurt to garnish

Method

1 Choose your preferred blend function, if required. Otherwise decide on your consistency at the end of cooking and then blend.

2 If your soup maker has a browning function, add the olive oil and onions first and leave to brown for a few minutes.

3 Add all the ingredients, except the milk, to the soup maker. Cover and leave to cook on high for 40 minutes. Ensure all the ingredients are well combined, tender and piping hot. Blend to your preferred consistency (or leave your machine to do this as programmed). Stir in the milk and warm through for a further 5 minutes. Adjust the seasoning and serve with a spoonful of yogurt.

CHEFS NOTE
Garnish with some fresh corriander/ cilantro and finely chopped red chilli if you wish.

CURRIED PARSNIP SOUP

Ingredients

- 1 tbsp olive oil
- 6 spring onions/scallions, chopped
- 1 large onion, peeled and chopped
- 2 large parsnips, peeled and chopped

- 1lt/4 cups vegetable stock/broth
- 3 tsp curry powder
- Salt and pepper
- Crushed chillies to garnish (optional)

Method

1 Choose your preferred blend function, if required. Otherwise decide on your consistency at the end of cooking and then blend.

2 If your soup maker has a browning function, add the olive oil, spring onions and onions first and leave to brown for a few minutes

3 Add all the ingredients to the soup maker except the crushed chillies. Cover and leave to cook on high for 40 minutes. Ensure all the ingredients are well combined, tender and piping hot. Blend to your preferred consistency (or leave your machine to do this as programmed). Adjust the seasoning and serve, garnished with the crushed chillies.

CHEFS NOTE
For a richer soup, add some cream just before serving.

CREAM OF SPINACH SOUP

Ingredients

- 50g/2oz butter
- 1 medium onion, peeled and chopped
- 2 garlic cloves, peeled and chopped
- 1 medium potato, peeled and chopped
- 500ml/2 cups vegetable stock/broth
- 500ml/2 cups milk
- 450g/1lb fresh spinach, roughly chopped
- Grated zest of ½ lemon
- Salt and pepper
- Grated nutmeg, to taste
- 3 tbsp double cream, to serve

Method

1 Choose your preferred blend function, if required. Otherwise decide on your consistency at the end of cooking and then blend.

2 If your soup maker has a browning function, add the butter, garlic and onions first and leave to brown for a few minutes.

3 Add all the ingredients, except the cream and nutmeg, to the soup maker. Cover and leave to cook on high for 30 minutes. Ensure all the ingredients are well combined, tender and piping hot. Blend to your preferred consistency (or leave your machine to do this as programmed). Adjust the seasoning and add a little nutmeg to taste. Serve with a generous swirl of cream.

CHEFS NOTE
This recipe also works with other leafy greens like chard or kale instead of spinach.

ASPARAGUS AND AUBERGINE SOUP

Ingredients

- 1 tbsp olive oil
- 1 large onion, peeled and chopped
- 300g/11oz asparagus tips, chopped
- ½ aubergine/eggplant, peeled and chopped

- 1 medium potato, peeled and chopped
- 750ml/3 cups vegetable stock/broth
- 1 tsp sundried tomato puree/paste
- Salt & pepper

Method

1 Choose your preferred blend function, if required. Otherwise decide on your consistency at the end of cooking and then blend.

2 If your soup maker has a browning function, add the olive oil and onions first and leave to brown for a few minutes.

3 Add all the ingredients to the soup maker. Cover and leave to cook on high for 40 minutes. Ensure all the ingredients are well combined, tender and piping hot. Blend to your preferred consistency (or leave your machine to do this as programmed). Adjust the seasoning and serve.

CHEFS NOTE

Asparagus is a lovely seasonal vegetable.

POTATO AND PEA SOUP

Ingredients

- 1 tbsp olive oil
- 1 medium onion, peeled and chopped
- 2 large potatoes, peeled and chopped
- 1lt/4 cups vegetable stock/broth
- 350g/12oz frozen peas
- 1 tbsp fresh mint, chopped

Method

1 Choose your preferred blend function, if required. Otherwise decide on your consistency at the end of cooking and then blend.

2 If your soup maker has a browning function, add the olive oil and onions first and leave to brown for a few minutes.

3 Add all the ingredients to the soup maker. Cover and leave to cook on high for 30 minutes. Ensure all the ingredients are well combined, tender and piping hot. Blend to your preferred consistency (or leave your machine to do this as programmed). Adjust the seasoning and serve.

CHEFS NOTE
Adjust the mint quantity to suit your own taste.

EASY CARROT AND CORIANDER SOUP

Ingredients

- 1 tbsp olive oil
- 1 medium onion, peeled and chopped
- 1 tsp ground coriander/cilantro
- 750ml/3 cups vegetable stock/broth

- 4 large carrots, peeled and chopped
- 1 small potato, peeled and chopped
- 250ml/1 cup fresh cream
- Salt and pepper

Method

1 Choose your preferred blend function, if required. Otherwise decide on your consistency at the end of cooking and then blend.

2 If your soup maker has a browning function, add the olive oil and onions first and leave to brown for a few minutes.

3 Add all the ingredients, except the cream, to the soup maker. Cover and leave to cook on high for 30 minutes. Ensure all the ingredients are well combined, tender and piping hot. Blend to your preferred consistency (or leave your machine to do this as programmed). Add the cream. Adjust the seasoning and serve.

CHEFS NOTE
Garnish each serving with a sprinkling of fresh, chopped coriander leaves.

SPROUT SOUP

Ingredients

- 2 tbsp olive oil
- 1 medium onion, peeled and chopped
- 450g/1lb Brussels sprouts, trimmed and halved
- 750ml/3 cups vegetable stock/broth

- 120ml/½ cup crème fraîche or sour cream
- Freshly ground nutmeg
- Salt and pepper

Method

1 Choose your preferred blend function, if required. Otherwise decide on your consistency at the end of cooking and then blend.

2 If your soup maker has a browning function, add the olive oil and onions first and leave to brown for a few minutes.

3 Add all the ingredients, except the crème fraîche and the nutmeg, to the soup maker. Cover and leave to cook on high for 20 minutes. Ensure all the ingredients are well combined, tender and piping hot. Blend to your preferred consistency (or leave your machine to do this as programmed). Pour in the crème fraîche, stir, and leave to warm through for a further 2-3 minutes. Add the nutmeg, adjust the seasoning and serve.

CHEFS NOTE
Brussels sprouts are a great source of Vitamins C & K.

GREEN SUMMER SOUP

Ingredients

- Knob of butter
- 2 stalks celery, chopped
- 4 spring onions/scallions, chopped
- ½ large cucumber, chopped

- 1lt/4 cups vegetable stock/broth
- 75g/3oz watercress
- 2 tbsp crème fraîche or sour cream
- Salt and freshly ground black pepper

Method

1 Choose your preferred blend function, if required. Otherwise decide on your consistency at the end of cooking and then blend.

2 If your soup maker has a browning function, add the butter and spring onions first and leave to brown for a few minutes.

3 Add all the ingredients, except the watercress and crème fraîche, to the soup maker. Cover and leave to cook for 20 minutes. Add the watercress and cook for a further 2 or 3 minutes. Ensure all the ingredients are well combined, tender and piping hot. Blend to your preferred consistency (or leave your machine to do this as programmed). Stir in the crème fraîche, adjust the seasoning and serve.

CHEFS NOTE
This delicious soup can be served hot or cold – ideal for a summer day and for picnics.

PEA AND LEEK SOUP

Ingredients

- 1 tbsp olive oil
- 1 medium leek, sliced
- 1 clove garlic, peeled and chopped
- 1 medium potato, peeled and chopped
- 750ml/3 cups vegetable stock/broth
- 450g/1lb frozen peas
- Salt and pepper
- 1 Little Gem lettuce, shredded

Method

1 Choose your preferred blend function, if required. Otherwise decide on your consistency at the end of cooking and then blend.

2 If your soup maker has a browning function, add the olive oil, leeks and garlic first and leave to brown for a few minutes.

3 Add all the ingredients, except the lettuce, to the soup maker. Cover and leave to cook on high for 30 minutes. Ensure all the ingredients are well combined, tender and piping hot. Blend to your preferred consistency (or leave your machine to do this as programmed). Add the shredded lettuce, adjust the seasoning and serve.

CHEFS NOTE
Use any type of firm lettuce you have to hand.

CHILLI BEAN SOUP

Ingredients

- 2 tbsp vegetable oil
- 1 medium onion, peeled and chopped
- 1 clove garlic, crushed
- 1 400g/14oz tin mixed beans, drained & rinsed
- 1 stalk celery, chopped

- 2 tsp dried mixed herbs
- 1 tsp dried crushed chilli
- 1 400g/14oz tin chopped tomatoes
- 750ml/3 cups vegetable stock/broth
- Crème fraiche/soured cream to serve (optional)

Method

1 Choose your preferred blend function, if required. Otherwise decide on your consistency at the end of cooking and then blend.

2 If your soup maker has a browning function, add the olive oil, onions and garlic first and leave to brown for a few minutes.

3 Add all the ingredients to the soup maker except the crème fraiche. Cover and leave to cook on high for 30 minutes. Ensure all the ingredients are well combined, tender and piping hot. Blend to your preferred consistency (or leave your machine to do this as programmed). Adjust the seasoning and serve with a spoonful of crème fraiche.

CHEFS NOTE
Try also with other tinned beans, e.g. kidney beans or butter beans.

COURGETTE AND PARMESAN SOUP

Ingredients

- 2 tbsp olive oil
- 1 tbsp chopped garlic
- 4 medium courgettes/zucchini, chopped
- Salt and pepper

- 750ml/3 cups vegetable stock/broth
- 60ml/¼ cup single cream
- 1 tbsp Parmesan cheese, grated

Method

1 Choose your preferred blend function, if required. Otherwise decide on your consistency at the end of cooking and then blend.

2 If your soup maker has a browning function, add the olive oil, garlic and courgettes first and leave to brown for 5 minutes.

3 Add all the ingredients, except the cream and Parmesan, to the soup maker. Cover and leave to cook for 20 minutes. Ensure all the ingredients are well combined, tender and piping hot. Blend to your preferred consistency (or leave your machine to do this as programmed). Stir in the cream and most of the Parmesan. Adjust the seasoning and serve sprinkled with the remaining Parmesan.

CHEFS NOTE
Delicious and refreshing served with a green salad and warm, crusty bread.

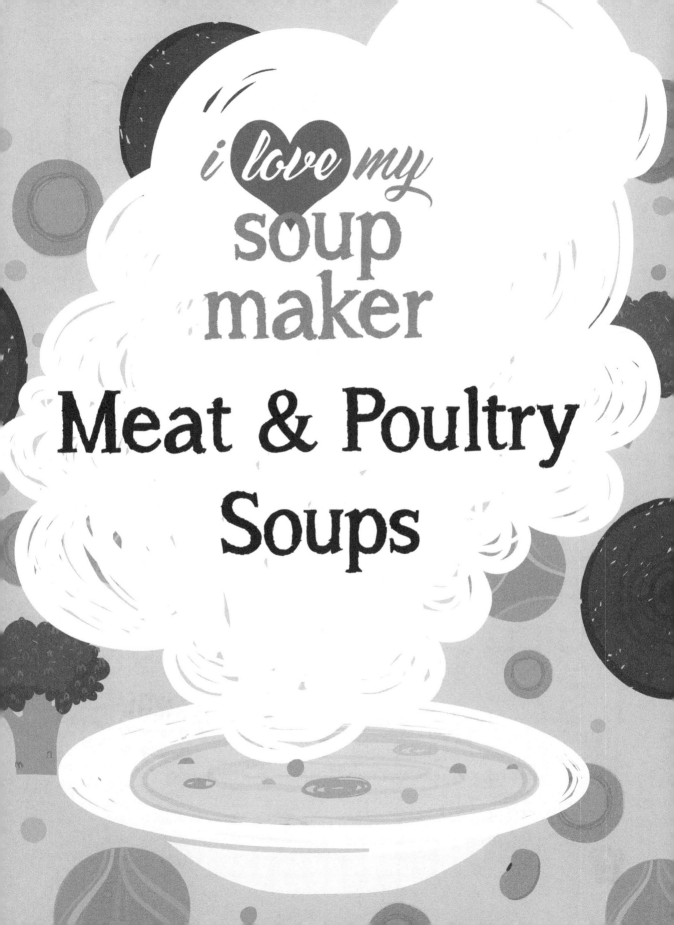

CHICKEN AND CHEESE SOUP

Ingredients

- 1 tbsp olive oil
- 225g/8oz cooked chicken breasts, chopped
- 1 medium onion, peeled and chopped
- 3 garlic cloves crushed
- 1 medium green bell pepper, de-seeded and chopped
- 1 400g/14oz tin chopped tomatoes

- 750ml/3 cups chicken stock
- 1 tbsp fresh basil, chopped
- 2 tsp fresh oregano, chopped
- Pinch of crushed chilli
- 125g/4oz small soup pasta
- 1 tbsp Parmesan cheese, grated, plus extra for garnish

Method

1 Choose your preferred blend function, if required. Otherwise decide on your consistency at the end of cooking and then blend.

2 Use cooked chicken in this recipe. If your soup maker has a browning function add the olive oil, onion and garlic and leave to brown for a few minutes.

3 Add all the ingredients, except the cheese and basil to the soup maker. Cover and leave to cook on high for 30 minutes. Ensure all the ingredients are well combined, tender and piping hot. Blend to your preferred consistency (or leave your machine to do this as programmed). Stir in the parmesan.

Adjust the seasoning and serve, garnished with fresh basil.

CHEFS NOTE
If you find the soup too thick, add a little more chicken stock until it's the consistency you want.

POTATO AND BACON SOUP

Ingredients

- 1 tbsp olive oil
- 5 slices back bacon
- 1 medium onion, peeled and chopped
- 3 cloves garlic, crushed
- 6 medium potatoes, peeled and chopped
- 1lt/4 cups chicken stock

- 1½ tsp salt
- 1 tsp ground pepper
- 250ml/1 cup single cream
- 2 tbsp mature cheddar cheese, grated, to garnish

Method

1 Choose your preferred blend function, if required. Otherwise decide on your consistency at the end of cooking and then blend.

2 If your machine has a browning function add the olive oil, onions and garlic and cook for a few minutes.

3 Fry the bacon in a pan until crisp, and chop.

4 Add all the ingredients to the soup maker except the cheese, cream and bacon. Cover and leave to cook on high for 40 minutes. Ensure all the ingredients are well combined, tender and piping hot. Blend to your preferred consistency (or leave your machine to do this as programmed). Adjust the seasoning and ladle into bowls.

5 Stir through the cream, top with the chopped bacon and some grated cheese.

CHEFS NOTE
This soup will keep well in the fridge for several days.

EASY CHICKEN NOODLE SOUP

Ingredients

- 75g/3oz dry noodles
- 1 carrot, peeled & chopped
- 1lt/4 cups chicken stock
- 200g/7oz sweetcorn
- 1 large potato, peeled and chopped
- 200g/7oz cooked chicken, shredded
- Salt & pepper to taste

Method

1 Choose your preferred blend function, if required. Otherwise decide on your consistency at the end of cooking and then blend.

2 Add all the ingredients to the soup maker. Cover and leave to cook on high until all the ingredients are well combined, tender and piping hot. Blend to your preferred consistency (or leave your machine to do this as programmed).

3 Adjust the seasoning & serve.

CHEFS NOTE
Try also with parsnips instead of potatoes and garnish with basil.

HAM SOUP

Ingredients

- 1 tbsp olive oil
- 1 medium onions, peeled and chopped
- 2 cloves garlic, crushed
- 225g/8oz honey roasted ham, cubed

- 750ml/3 cups chicken stock/broth
- 1 tsp paprika
- Black pepper to taste
- 1 400g/14oz tin chopped tomatoes

Method

1 Choose your preferred blend function, if required. Otherwise decide on your consistency at the end of cooking and then blend.

2 If your soup maker has a browning function, add the olive oil and onions first and leave to brown for a few minutes.

3 Add all the ingredients to the soup maker. Cover and leave to cook on high for 40 minutes. Ensure all the ingredients are well combined, tender and piping hot. Blend to your preferred consistency (or leave your machine to do this as programmed). Adjust the seasoning and serve.

CHEFS NOTE

If you can, try making the stock from a ham bone - this will impart a more intense flavour.

BEEF AND BARLEY SOUP

Ingredients

- 1 tbsp olive oil
- 450g/1lb cooked stewing steak, cubed
- 1 medium onion, chopped
- 2 cloves garlic, crushed
- Salt and pepper

- 1lt/4 cups beef stock
- 2 stalks celery, chopped
- 1 medium potato, peeled and chopped
- 2 medium carrots, peeled and chopped
- 200g/7oz pearl barley, rinsed

Method

1 Choose your preferred blend function, if required. Otherwise decide on your consistency at the end of cooking and then blend.

2 Cook the meat in advance. If your soup maker has a browning function add the olive oil, onions and garlic first and sauté for a few minutes.

3 Add all the ingredients to the soup maker. Cover and leave to cook for an hour, or until the meat is tender. Blend to your preferred consistency (or leave your machine to do this as programmed). Adjust the seasoning and serve.

CHEFS NOTE
Add any vegetables you like to this rich, tasty soup!

SIMPLE SAUSAGE AND BEAN SOUP

Ingredients

- 1 tsp olive oil
- 225g/8oz cooked pork sausages, sliced
- 1 400g/14oz tin chopped tomatoes
- 750ml/3 cups chicken stock/broth
- 1 tsp dried mixed herbs

- ¼ tsp pepper
- 1 400g/14oz tin cannellini beans, rinsed and drained
- 1 400g/14oz tin chickpeas, rinsed and drained

Method

1 Choose your preferred blend function, if required. Otherwise decide on your consistency at the end of cooking and then blend.

2 Cook the sausages in advance.

3 Add all the ingredients to the soup maker. Cover and leave to cook on high for 30 minutes. Ensure all the ingredients are well combined, tender and piping hot. Blend to your preferred consistency (or leave your machine to do this as programmed). Adjust the seasoning and serve.

CHEFS NOTE
Chorizo sausages also make a good alternative to plain pork.

CREAMY CHICKEN RICE SOUP

Ingredients

- 50g/2oz butter
- ½ onion, peeled and chopped
- 225g/8oz chicken breasts, cooked and sliced
- 125g/4oz long grain rice, rinsed
- 1 stalk celery, chopped
- 1 medium carrot, peeled and chopped
- 750ml/3 cups chicken stock
- 1 tbsp fresh chopped thyme
- 250ml/1 cup whole milk
- 120ml/½ cup white wine
- Salt and pepper

Method

1 Choose your preferred blend function, if required. Otherwise decide on your consistency at the end of cooking and then blend.

2 Cook the chicken in advance.

3 If your soup maker has a browning function add the butter and onions first and leave to brown for a few minutes.

4 Add all the ingredients to the soup maker. Cover and leave to cook on high for 40 minutes. Ensure all the ingredients are well combined, tender and piping hot. Blend to your preferred consistency (or leave your machine to do this as programmed). Adjust the seasoning and serve.

CHEFS NOTE
Try using sage in place of thyme to give a different flavour.

BEEF AND VEGETABLE SOUP

Ingredients

- 1 tbsp olive oil
- 1 medium onion, peeled and chopped
- 225g/8oz minced/ground beef, cooked
- 750ml/3 cups beef stock
- 2 medium carrots, peeled and chopped
- 1 stalk celery, chopped
- 1 clove garlic, crushed
- 1 400g/14oz tin chopped tomatoes
- 1 medium potato, peeled and chopped
- 100g/3½oz tinned sweetcorn, drained
- 100g/3½oz green beans
- 100g/3½oz peas
- Salt and pepper

Method

1 Choose your preferred blend function, if required. Otherwise decide on your consistency at the end of cooking and then blend.

2 Cook the mince in advance.

3 If your soup maker has a browning function add the olive oil and onions and leave to brown for a few minutes.

4 Add all the ingredients to the soup maker. Cover and leave to cook on high for 30 minutes. Ensure all the ingredients are well combined, tender and piping hot. Blend to your preferred consistency (or leave your machine to do this as programmed). Adjust the seasoning and serve.

CHEFS NOTE
Add more stock if you want to alter the consistency of this soup

BEEF STOCK AND ONION SOUP

Ingredients

- 2 large onions, peeled and sliced
- 1 clove garlic, crushed
- 1lt/4 cups beef stock/broth
- 1 tbsp fresh chopped thyme
- 1 tbsp Worcestershire sauce
- Salt and pepper
- 2 tbsp Parmesan cheese, grated
- 2 tbsp Gruyere cheese, grated, to garnish

Method

1 Choose your preferred blend function, if required. Otherwise decide on your consistency at the end of cooking and then blend.

2 If your soup maker has a browning function, add the olive oil and onions first and leave to brown for a few minutes

3 Add all the ingredients except the Parmesan and Gruyere to the soup maker. Cover and leave to cook on high for 30 minutes. Ensure all the ingredients are well combined, tender and piping hot. Blend to your preferred consistency (or leave your machine to do this as programmed). Stir in the Parmesan. Adjust the seasoning and serve topped with a sprinkling of Gruyere.

CHEFS NOTE
For extra French flavour, add a generous dash of brandy to the soup.

SQUASH AND SAUSAGE SOUP

Ingredients

- 1 tbsp olive oil
- 3 sausages, cooked and sliced
- 1 medium onion, peeled and chopped
- 2 cloves garlic, crushed
- 1 medium red bell pepper, de-seeded and chopped
- 1lt/4 cups chicken stock/broth

- 400g/14oz butternut squash, peeled and cubed
- 225g/8oz kale, roughly chopped
- 200g/7oz tin cannellini beans, drained and rinsed
- Salt and pepper to taste
- Parmesan cheese, grated, to garnish

Method

1 Choose your preferred blend function, if required. Otherwise decide on your consistency at the end of cooking and then blend.

2 Cook the sausages in advance.

3 If your soup machine has a browning function add the olive oil and onions first and leave to brown for a few minutes.

4 Add all the ingredients to the soup maker. Cover and leave to cook on high for 30 minutes. Ensure all the ingredients are well combined, tender and piping hot. Blend to your preferred consistency (or leave your machine to do this as programmed). Adjust the seasoning and serve with a sprinkling of Parmesan.

CHEFS NOTE
Be sparing with the seasoning until you taste – you may need less than usual, depending on the sausages you use.

HAM AND POTATO SOUP

Ingredients

- 1 tbsp butter
- 1 medium onion, peeled and chopped
- 2 stalks celery, chopped
- 2 medium potatoes, peeled and chopped
- 1 small carrot, peeled and chopped

- 150g/5oz cooked ham, diced
- 500ml/2 cups chicken stock/broth
- 500ml/2 cups milk
- Salt and pepper
- Mature Cheddar cheese, grated, to garnish

Method

1 Choose your preferred blend function, if required. Otherwise decide on your consistency at the end of cooking and then blend.

2 If your soup maker has a browning function, add the butter, onions and celery first and leave to brown for a few minutes.

3 Add all the ingredients to the soup maker excpet the cheese.. Cover and leave to cook on high for 30 minutes. Ensure all the ingredients are well combined, tender and piping hot. Blend to your preferred consistency (or leave your machine to do this as programmed). Adjust the seasoning and serve garnished with grated cheese.

CHEFS NOTE
You can use either full fat or semi-skimmed milk in this recipe. Alternatively, for a more luxurious soup, use half the quantity of milk, and stir through some double cream just before you serve.

BACON SQUASH SOUP

Ingredients

- 2 tbsp olive oil
- 1 medium butternut squash, peeled, de-seeded and chopped
- 1 medium onion, peeled and chopped
- 1 medium red bell pepper, de-seeded and chopped
- 6 slices back bacon, cooked and finely chopped
- 2 cloves garlic, crushed
- Salt and pepper
- ½ tsp dried thyme
- 1lt/4 cups chicken stock

Method

1 Choose your preferred blend function, if required. Otherwise decide on your consistency at the end of cooking and then blend.

2 If your soup maker has a browning function, add the oil, squash, onions, pepper and leave to brown for ten minutes. If your machine doesn't brown, roast these ingredients in the oven for 30-40 minutes at 180C/350F/Gas4.

3 Add all the ingredients to the soup maker. Cover and leave to cook on high for 30 minutes. Ensure all the ingredients are well combined, tender and piping hot. Blend to your preferred consistency (or leave your machine to do this as programmed). Adjust the seasoning and serve.

CHEFS NOTE
This is great topped with chopped chives and crumbled goat's cheese.

CREAM OF CHICKEN SOUP

Ingredients

- 2 tsp olive oil
- 450g/1lb chicken boneless thighs, cooked and chopped
- 1 medium onion, peeled and chopped
- 1 large potato, peeled and chopped

- ½ medium cauliflower, chopped
- 750ml/3 cups chicken stock
- 120ml/½ cup milk
- 120ml/½ cup double cream

Method

1 Choose your preferred blend function, if required. Otherwise decide on your consistency at the end of cooking and then blend.

2 Cook the chicken in advance.

3 If your soup maker has a browning function add the olive oil and onions first and leave to brown for a few minutes.

4 Add all the ingredients except the cream to the soup maker. Cover and leave to cook on high for 30 minutes. Ensure all the ingredients are well combined, tender and piping hot. Blend to your preferred consistency (or leave your machine to do this as programmed). Stir in the cream, adjust the seasoning and serve.

CHEFS NOTE
Parmesan and breadcrumbs make lovely garnishes for this soup.

LEFT OVER TURKEY SOUP

Ingredients

- 1 tbsp olive oil
- 1 large onion, peeled and sliced
- 1 medium red pepper, de-seeded and sliced
- 3 tbsp long grain rice
- 1lt/4 cups chicken stock

- 250g/8oz cooked turkey meat, chopped
- 400g/14oz tin chickpeas, drained and rinsed
- Handful of fresh parsley, roughly chopped

Method

1 Choose your preferred blend function, if required. Otherwise decide on your consistency at the end of cooking and then blend.

2 Cook the turkey in advance.

3 If your soup maker has a browning function, add the olive oil and onions first and leave to brown for a few minutes.

4 Add all the ingredients except the parsley to the soup maker. Cover and leave to cook on high for 30 minutes. Ensure all the ingredients are well combined, tender and piping hot. Blend to your preferred consistency (or leave your machine to do this as programmed). Stir in the parsley, adjust the seasoning and serve.

CHEFS NOTE

This is a great and tasty way to use up leftover turkey at Christmas. Plus, you can freeze this soup for up to a month.

SCOTCH BROTH

Ingredients

- 1 tbsp olive oil
- 1 medium leek, chopped
- 1 stalk celery, chopped
- 1 medium onion, peeled and sliced
- 300g/11oz leftover roast lamb, chopped
- Salt and pepper

- 1 medium carrot, peeled and chopped
- 1lt/4 cups lamb or beef stock
- 1 small swede, peeled and chopped
- 1 large potato, peeled and chopped
- 75g/3oz pearl barley

Method

1 Choose your preferred blend function, if required. Otherwise decide on your consistency at the end of cooking and then blend.

2 Cook the lamb in advance.

3 If your soup maker has a browning function, add the olive oil, leeks, celery and onions first and leave to brown for a few minutes.

4 Add all the ingredients to the soup maker. Cover and leave to cook on high for 30 minutes. Ensure all the ingredients are well combined, tender and piping hot. Blend to your preferred consistency (or leave your machine to do this as programmed). Adjust the seasoning and serve.

CHEFS NOTE
This is a great way to use leftover roast meat.

BACON AND CHESTNUT SOUP

Ingredients

- 1 tbsp olive oil
- 1 medium onion, peeled and chopped
- 5 rashers streaky bacon, cooked and chopped
- 1 stalk celery, chopped
- 2 medium carrots, peeled and chopped

- 200g/7oz vacuum-packed chestnuts
- 1lt/4 cups chicken or vegetable stock/broth
- Salt and freshly ground black pepper
- Few sprigs of thyme, to garnish

Method

1 Choose your preferred blend function, if required. Otherwise decide on your consistency at the end of cooking and then blend.

2 Cook the bacon in advance.

3 If your soup maker has a browning function, add the olive oil and onions first and leave to brown for 10 minutes.

4 Add all the ingredients except the thyme sprigs to the soup maker. Cover and leave to cook on high for 30 minutes. Ensure all the ingredients are well combined, tender and piping hot. Blend to your preferred consistency (or leave your machine to do this as programmed). Adjust the seasoning, garnish with the fresh sprigs of thyme and serve.

CHEFS NOTE

This soup makes a delicious starter to Christmas dinner. You can even make it well in advance, since it will freeze for up to three months.

PANCETTA AND BEAN SOUP

Ingredients

- 1 tbsp olive oil
- 100g/3½ oz pancetta, cooked and diced
- 1 medium onion, peeled and chopped
- 2 small carrots, peeled and chopped
- 2 stalks celery, chopped
- 1 clove garlic, crushed

- 2 medium tomatoes, diced
- 1 tbsp tomato puree/paste
- 1lt/4 cups chicken stock/broth
- 125g/4oz pearl barley
- 1 400g/14oz tin cannellini beans

Method

1 Choose your preferred blend function, if required. Otherwise decide on your consistency at the end of cooking and then blend.

2 Cook the pancetta in advance.

3 If your soup maker has a browning function, add the olive oil, onions and garlic first and brown for a few minutes:

4 Add all the ingredients to the soup maker. Cover and leave to cook on high for 30 minutes. Ensure all the ingredients are well combined, tender and piping hot. Blend to your preferred consistency (or leave your machine to do this as programmed). Adjust the seasoning and serve.

CHEFS NOTE
If you don't have pancetta, smoked bacon is a good substitute.

PEA AND HAM SOUP

Ingredients

- 1 tbsp olive oil
- 2 medium onions, peeled and chopped
- 1lt/4 cups chicken or vegetable stock/broth

- 2 medium carrots, peeled and chopped
- 450g/1lb frozen peas
- 150g/5oz cooked ham, shredded

Method

1 Choose your preferred blend function, if required. Otherwise decide on your consistency at the end of cooking and then blend.

2 If your soup maker has a browning function, add the olive oil and onions first and leave to brown for a few minutes.

3 Add all the ingredients to the soup maker. Cover and leave to cook on high for 30 minutes. Ensure all the ingredients are well combined, tender and piping hot. Blend to your preferred consistency (or leave your machine to do this as programmed). Adjust the seasoning and serve.

CHEFS NOTE
Use any kind of ham or cooked gammon you have to hand.

CHICKEN AND COCONUT SOUP

Ingredients

- 2 tbsp olive oil
- 2 chicken breast fillets, cooked and cut into strips
- 1 medium onion, peeled and chopped
- 1 clove garlic, crushed
- 1 tsp ground corriander/cilantro
- 1 tsp ground cumin
- 750ml/3 cups chicken stock
- 250ml/1 cup coconut milk
- Salt and freshly ground black pepper
- Handful of fresh basil leaves, chopped

Method

1 Choose your preferred blend function, if required. Otherwise decide on your consistency at the end of cooking and then blend.

2 Cook the chicken in advance.

3 If your soup maker has a browning function add the olive oil, onions and garlic first. Leave to brown for a few minutes.

4 Add all the ingredients except the basil to the soup maker. Cover and leave to cook on high for 30 minutes. Ensure all the ingredients are well combined, tender and piping hot. Blend to your preferred consistency (or leave your machine to do this as programmed). Adjust the seasoning, stir in the basil leaves and serve.

CHEFS NOTE
Try also substituting coriander leaves for basil.

COCK-A-LEEKIE SOUP

Ingredients

- 350g/12oz boneless chicken thighs, cooked and chopped
- 1 medium onion, peeled and chopped
- 2 medium leeks, chopped

- 1lt/4 cups chicken stock
- 50g/2oz pearl barley
- Salt and pepper

Method

1 Choose your preferred blend function, if required. Otherwise decide on your consistency at the end of cooking and then blend.

2 Cook the chicken in advance,.

3 If your soup maker has a browning function add the olive oil and onions first and eave to cook for a few minutes.

4 Add all the ingredients to the soup maker. Cover and leave to cook on high for 30 minutes. Ensure all the ingredients are well combined, tender and piping hot. Blend to your preferred consistency (or leave your machine to do this as programmed). Adjust the seasoning, and serve.

CHEFS NOTE
Add fresh herbs to this tasty soup for even greater flavour.

CHICKEN NOODLE SOUP

Ingredients

- 350g/12oz boneless chicken thighs, cooked and chopped
- 1 medium onion, peeled and chopped
- 1 large carrot, peeled and chopped
- 1 stalk celery, trimmed
- 2 medium leeks, chopped
- 125g/4oz rice noodles
- 1lt/4 cups chicken stock
- Handful of spring onions/scallions to garnish

Method

1 Choose your preferred blend function, if required – chunky is recommended for this soup. Otherwise decide on your consistency at the end of cooking and then blend.

2 Cook the chicken in advance.

3 If your soup maker has a browning function add the olive oil and onions first and leave to cook for a few minutes.

4 Add all the ingredients, except the spring onions, to the soup maker. Cover and leave to cook on high for 30 minutes. Ensure all the ingredients are well combined, tender and piping hot. Blend on the chunky setting (or leave your machine to do this as programmed). Adjust the seasoning, and serve with the spring onions over the top.

CHEFS NOTE
Cut the spring onions into ribbons by finely slicing the white bulbs lengthways.

LEFTOVER MEAT SOUP

Ingredients

- 1 tbsp olive oil
- 1 medium onion, peeled and chopped
- 1 large carrot, peeled and chopped
- 1 stalk celery, chopped
- 1 clove garlic, crushed
- 1 400g/14oz tin kidney beans, drained and rinsed

- 1 400g/14oz tin tomatoes
- 750ml/3 cups chicken stock/broth
- 200g/7oz cooked meat, chopped or shredded
- Salt and freshly ground black pepper
- Handful of parsley leaves, to garnish

Method

1 Choose your preferred blend function, if required – chunky is recommended for this soup. Otherwise decide on your consistency at the end of cooking and then blend.

2 If your soup maker has a browning function, add the olive oil and onions first and leave to brown for a few minutes.

3 Add all the ingredients, except the meat and parsley, to the soup maker. Cover and leave to cook on high for 20 minutes. Ensure all the ingredients are well combined, tender and piping hot. Blend to your preferred consistency (or leave your machine to do this as programmed). Stir in the chopped meat and leave to heat through for another few minutes. Adjust the seasoning, and serve garnished with parsley.

CHEFS NOTE

Any leftover cooked meat will do for this recipe. Make sure the soup is piping hot before serving.

TURKEY AND MUSHROOM SOUP

Ingredients

- 1 tbsp olive oil
- 1 medium onion, peeled and chopped
- 1lt/4 cups chicken stock/broth
- 2 tsp chopped fresh mixed herbs, e.g. sage and thyme
- Salt and freshly ground black pepper
- 250g/8oz mushrooms, sliced
- 120ml/½ cup milk
- 125g/4oz cooked turkey meat, finely chopped or shredded

Method

1 Choose your preferred blend function, if required – chunky is recommended. Otherwise decide on your consistency at the end of cooking and then blend.

2 Cook the turkey meat in advance.

3 If your soup maker has a browning function, add the olive oil and onions first and leave to brown for a few minutes.

4 Add all the ingredients, except the turkey to the soup maker. Cover and leave to cook on high for 20 minutes. Ensure all the ingredients are well combined, tender and piping hot. Blend to your preferred consistency (or leave your machine to do this as programmed). Stir in the turkey pieces and leave to warm through for a few minutes. Adjust the seasoning, and serve.

CHEFS NOTE
If you have leftover gravy, add about 120ml/½ cup to the mix before cooking – it will give the soup added richness and flavour.

BACON AND BUTTERBEAN SOUP

Ingredients

- 1 tbsp olive oil
- 1 medium onion, peeled and chopped
- 4 rashers smoked streaky bacon, cooked and chopped
- 750ml/3 cups chicken or vegetable stock

- 2 x 400g/14oz tins butterbeans, drained and rinsed
- 1 tbsp chopped sage
- Salt and freshly ground black pepper
- Fresh sage leaves, to garnish

Method

1 Choose your preferred blend function, if required – chunky is recommended for this soup. Otherwise decide on your consistency at the end of cooking and then blend.

2 If your soup maker has a browning function, add the olive oil and onions and leave to brown for 5 or 10 minutes.

3 Add all the ingredients to the soup maker. Cover and leave to cook on high for 20 minutes. Ensure all the ingredients are well combined, tender and piping hot. Blend to your preferred consistency (or leave your machine to do this as programmed). Adjust the seasoning, and serve. Garnish with a few fresh sage leaves.

CHEFS NOTE
If you like, add some more pieces of crisped bacon as garnish.

i love my soup maker

Fish & Seafood Soups

CULLEN SKINK

Ingredients

- Knob of butter
- 2 large potatoes, peeled and chopped
- 1 onion, peeled and chopped
- 300g/11oz smoked haddock, boneless & skinless
- 250ml/1 cup water (from poaching pan)

- 750ml/3 cups full fat or semi-skimmed milk
- 1 tsp salt
- 1 tsp black pepper
- 120ml/½ cup single cream

Method

1 Choose your preferred blend function, if required. Otherwise decide on your consistency at the end of cooking and then blend.

2 If your soup maker has a browning function, add the butter, onions and potatoes first and leave to brown for a few minutes.

3 In a pan, poach the haddock in water for 5-7 minutes, until fully cooked. Remove the haddock and strain the fish 'stock' that's left over.

4 Put the potatoes, onion and 250ml/1 cup of stock from the poached fish pan into the soup maker. Top up with the milk. Add the salt and pepper. Cover and leave to cook on high for 30 minutes.

5 Add the fish and warm for another couple of minutes. Ensure all the ingredients are well combined, tender and piping hot.

6 Blend on the smooth setting or serve this chunky as a more rustic dish.

7 Stir in cream to suit your taste and serve.

CHEFS NOTE
Unlike most soups, this one is not suitable for freezing.

CREAM OF CRAB SOUP

Ingredients

- Knob of butter
- ½ onion, peeled and chopped
- 250ml/1 cup chicken stock/broth
- ¼ tsp celery salt
- 1 dash freshly ground black pepper

- 750ml/3 cups milk
- 450g/1lb crabmeat, cooked and shredded
- Chopped fresh parsley to garnish

Method

1 Choose your preferred blend function, if required. Otherwise decide on your consistency at the end of cooking and then blend.

2 If your soup maker has a browning function, add the butter and onions first and leave to brown for a few minutes

3 Add all the ingredients, except the crabmeat and parsley, to the soup maker. Cover and leave to cook on high for 20 minutes. Fold in the crabmeat and leave to warm through for a further 3-5 minutes. Ensure all the ingredients are well combined, tender and piping hot. Blend to your preferred consistency (or leave your machine to do this as programmed). Adjust the seasoning and serve, garnished with parsley.

CHEFS NOTE
Use tinned crabmeat if you can't get fresh.

JAMBALAYA SOUP

Ingredients

- 1 tbsp olive oil
- 1 onion, peeled and chopped
- 1 stalk celery, chopped
- 2 garlic cloves, peeled and chopped
- 2 green chillies, de-seeded & chopped
- 2 tsp smoked paprika
- 250ml/1 cup tomato passata/sieved tomatoes

- 750ml/3 cups chicken stock/broth
- 350g/12oz sausages, cooked and sliced
- 1 red bell pepper, deseeded and chopped
- 1 green bell pepper, deseeded and chopped
- 125g/4oz long grain rice
- 225g/8oz prawns, cooked and shelled
- 1 tbsp flat leaf parsley, chopped

Method

1 Choose your preferred blend function, if required. Otherwise decide on your consistency at the end of cooking and then blend.

2 Cook the sausages and prawns in advance,.If your soup maker has a browning function, add the olive oil, onions and garlic first and leave to brown for a few minutes.

3 Add all the ingredients, except the prawns and parsley, to the soup maker. Cover and leave to cook on high for 40 minutes. Add the prawns and leave to heat through. Ensure all the ingredients are well combined, tender and piping hot. Blend to your preferred consistency (or leave your machine to do this as programmed).

4 Adjust the seasoning and serve, garnished with the parsley.

CHEFS NOTE
If you don't like your soup too spicy, use just one chilli.

HALIBUT CHOWDER

Ingredients

- 50g/2oz bacon, cooked & chopped
- 1 medium onion, peeled and chopped
- 750ml/3 cups fish stock/broth
- 2 medium potatoes, peeled and chopped
- 2 celery stalks, chopped
- 250ml/1 cup single cream

- 225g/8oz cooked halibut, boneless, skinless and chopped
- ½ tsp salt
- ¼ tsp ground white pepper
- 1 tbsp olive oil
- Chopped fresh chives to garnish

Method

1 Choose your preferred blend function, if required. Otherwise decide on your consistency at the end of cooking and then blend.

2 Cook the halibut in advance.

3 If your soup maker has a browning function, add the olive oil and onions first and leave to brown for a few minutes.

4 Add all the ingredients, except the cream and chives, to the soup maker. Cover and leave to cook on high for 30 minutes. Ensure all the ingredients are well combined, tender and piping hot. Blend to your preferred consistency (or leave your machine to do this as programmed). Stir in the cream, adjust the seasoning and serve garnished with chives.

CHEFS NOTE
This recipe works well with most fish, so feel free to experiment!

SMOKED HADDOCK SOUP

Ingredients

- 1 tbsp olive oil
- 1 medium onion, peeled and chopped
- 2 celery stalks, chopped
- 1lt/4 cups milk
- 4 medium potatoes, peeled and chopped
- 400g/14oz cooked smoked haddock fillets, boneless and skinless
- 200g/7oz frozen sweetcorn
- Salt and freshly ground black pepper
- 2 tbsp chopped fresh parsley

Method

1 Choose your preferred blend function, if required. Otherwise decide on your consistency at the end of cooking and then blend.

2 Cook the haddock in advance.

3 If your soup maker has a browning function, add the olive oil, onions and celery first and leave to brown for a few minutes.

4 Add all the ingredients to the soup maker. Cover and leave to cook on high for 20 minutes. Ensure all the ingredients are well combined, tender and piping hot. Blend to your preferred consistency (or leave your machine to do this as programmed). Adjust the seasoning and serve.

CHEFS NOTE
Serve this soup as a main course, with some warm crusty bread. Alternatively, serve smaller quantities as a starter.

SPICED SHRIMP SOUP

Ingredients

- 1 tbsp olive oil
- 1 medium onion, peeled and chopped
- 750ml/3 cups chicken stock/broth
- 120ml/½ cup white wine
- 2 celery stalks, chopped
- 2 tsp fresh, grated ginger

- 1 tsp soy sauce
- 1 small head broccoli, chopped
- 225g/8oz cooked shrimp/prawns
- 1 tbsp fresh corriander/cilantro, chopped
- Pinch crushed chillies

Method

1 Choose your preferred blend function, if required. Otherwise decide on your consistency at the end of cooking and then blend.

2 Cook the shrimp in advance.

3 If your soup maker has a browning function, add the olive oil and onions first and leave to brown for a few minutes.

4 Add all the ingredients, except the shrimp and coriander, to the soup maker. Cover and leave to cook on high for 30 minutes. Add the shrimp and leave for a further 3 minutes or so to warm through. Ensure all the ingredients are well combined, tender and piping hot. Blend to your preferred consistency (or leave your machine to do this as programmed.

5 Stir in the coriander. Season and serve.

CHEFS NOTE
Peel the stems of the broccoli, finely chop and use them in the soup along with the florets.

CHUNKY COD SOUP

Ingredients

- 2 tbsp olive oil
- 2 medium onions, peeled and chopped
- 2 stalks celery, chopped
- 1lt/4 cups fish stock/broth
- 2 medium carrots, peeled and chopped
- 2 large potatoes, peeled and chopped
- 150g/5oz green beans, chopped
- 2 medium courgettes/zucchini, chopped
- 1 yellow bell pepper, de-seeded and chopped
- 1 400g/14oz tin chopped tomatoes
- Salt and pepper
- 550g/1¼lb cod fillets, skinned, cooked and cut into strips
- Handful of flat leaf parsley, roughly chopped

Method

1 Choose your preferred blend function, if required. Otherwise decide on your consistency at the end of cooking and then blend.

2 Cook the cod in advance.

3 If your soup maker has a browning function, add the olive oil, onions and celery first and leave to brown for a few minutes.

4 Add all the ingredients, except the parsley, to the soup maker. Cover and leave to cook on high for 30 minutes. Ensure all the ingredients are well combined, tender and piping hot. Blend to your preferred consistency (or leave your machine to do this as programmed). Stir in the parsley, adjust the seasoning and serve.

CHEFS NOTE
Also delicious with other white fish such as haddock or coley.

SALMON AND POTATO SOUP

Ingredients

- 1 tbsp olive oil
- 2 stalks celery, chopped
- 1 medium onion, peeled and chopped
- 750ml/3 cups milk
- 1 can condensed cream of celery soup
- 1 tbsp fresh dill, chopped

- Pinch caraway seeds
- Salt and pepper
- 1 medium potato, peeled and chopped
- 175g/6oz salmon fillets, skinned, cooked and sliced

Method

1 Choose your preferred blend function, if required. Otherwise decide on your consistency at the end of cooking and then blend.

2 Cook the salmon in advance.

3 If your soup maker has a browning function, add the olive oil, onions and celery first and leave to brown for a few minutes.

4 Add all the ingredients to the soup maker. Cover and leave to cook on high for 30 minutes. Ensure all the ingredients are well combined, tender and piping hot. Blend to your preferred consistency (or leave your machine to do this as programmed). Adjust the seasoning and serve.

CHEFS NOTE
Add character to this tasty soup by crumbling some crisped, chopped bacon over the top when served.

COD AND CHORIZO SOUP

Ingredients

- 1 tbsp olive oil
- 1 medium onion, peeled and chopped
- 225g/8oz chorizo sausage, chopped
- 1 garlic clove, crushed
- 225g/8oz cooked cod fillet, skinned, chopped
- 1 red chilli, de-seeded and chopped
- 1 tbsp basil leaves, chopped

- 75g/3oz long grain rice
- 750ml/3 cups tomato passata/sieved tomatoes
- 250ml/1 cup water
- 1 400g/14oz tin kidney beans, drained and rinsed
- Salt and pepper to taste
- 1 lemon, sliced, to garnish

Method

1 Choose your preferred blend function, if required. Otherwise decide on your consistency at the end of cooking and then blend.

2 Cook the cod in advance.

3 If your soup maker has a browning function, add the olive oil, onions and chorizo first and leave to brown for a few minutes.

4 Add all the ingredients to the soup maker. Cover and leave to cook on high for 30 minutes. Ensure all the ingredients are well combined, tender and piping hot. Blend to your preferred consistency (or leave your machine to do this as programmed).

Adjust the seasoning and serve garnished with lemon wedges.

CHEFS NOTE
Alternatively, you can use salami instead of chorizo.

CREAMY MONKFISH AND CARROT SOUP

Ingredients

- 50g/2oz butter
- 1 medium onion, peeled and chopped
- 2 medium potatoes, peeled and chopped
- 2 medium carrots, peeled and chopped
- 750ml/3 cups chicken stock/broth
- 120ml/½ cup dry white wine

- 1 tsp dried thyme
- Salt and pepper
- 550g/1¼lb cooked monkfish, skinned and cut into strips
- 120ml/½ cup double cream
- 1 tbsp chopped flat leaf parsley to garnish

Method

1 Choose your preferred blend function, if required. Otherwise decide on your consistency at the end of cooking and then blend.

2 Cook the monkfish in advance.

3 If your soup maker has a browning function, add the butter and onions first and leave to brown for a few minutes.

4 Add all the ingredients except the cream and parsley to the soup maker. Cover and leave to cook on high for 30 minutes. Ensure all the ingredients are well combined, tender and piping hot. Blend to your preferred consistency (or leave your machine to do this as programmed). Stir in the cream, adjust the seasoning and serve garnished with chopped parsley.

CHEFS NOTE
If you can't obtain monkfish, haddock or cod is also delicious with this recipe.

EASY TUNA AND SWEETCORN SOUP

Ingredients

- Knob of butter
- 1 tbsp oil
- 1 medium onion, peeled and chopped
- 1 garlic clove, crushed
- 1 medium carrot, peeled and chopped
- 1 medium courgette/zucchini, chopped
- 250ml/1 cup tomato passata/sieved tomatoes
- 750ml/3 cups chicken stock/broth
- 1 tsp each dried basil
- 275g/10oz mushrooms, sliced
- 200g/7oz tinned sweetcorn
- 1 400g/14oz tin chickpeas, rinsed and drained
- 165g/5½oz tinned tuna, drained
- Salt and pepper
- 50g/2oz mature cheddar cheese, grated, to garnish
- Chopped corriander/cilantro, to garnish

Method

1 Choose your preferred blend function, if required. Otherwise decide on your consistency at the end of cooking and then blend.

2 If your soup maker has a browning function, add the butter, olive oil, onions and mushrooms first and leave to brown for a few minutes.

3 Add all the ingredients, to the soup maker except the cheese and coriander. Cover and leave to cook on high for 30 minutes. Ensure all the ingredients are well combined, tender and piping hot. Blend to your preferred consistency (or leave your machine to do this as programmed). Adjust the seasoning and serve.

4 Sprinkle each serving with grated cheese and a little fresh coriander.

CHEFS NOTE

For a spicier flavour, add a teaspoon of dried chilli to the soup!

TUNA AND BEAN SOUP

Ingredients

- 1 tbsp olive oil
- 1 medium onion, peeled and chopped
- 3 cloves garlic, peeled and chopped
- 1lt/4 cups chicken stock/broth
- 165g/5oz tinned tuna, drained

- 1 400g/14oz tin cannellini beans, drained and rinsed
- 1 handful kale, chopped
- 1 tbsp parmesan cheese, grated
- Salt and pepper to taste

Method

1 Choose your preferred blend function, if required. Otherwise decide on your consistency at the end of cooking and then blend.

2 If your soup maker has a browning function, add the olive oil, onions and garlic first and leave to brown for a few minutes.

3 Add all the ingredients except the cheese to the soup maker. Cover and leave to cook on high for 20 minutes. Ensure all the ingredients are well combined, tender and piping hot. Blend to your preferred consistency (or leave your machine to do this as programmed). Stir in the Parmesan until it melts. Adjust the seasoning and serve.

CHEFS NOTE
Feel free to replace the kale with Swiss chard, spinach or other leafy green.

CLAM CHOWDER

Ingredients

- Knob of butter
- 2 slices back bacon, cooked and chopped
- 1 medium onion, peeled and chopped
- 6 large clams
- 2 medium potatoes, peeled and chopped
- 2 cloves garlic, crushed
- 750ml/3 cups fish stock/broth

- 60ml/¼ cup dry white wine
- 1 tsp fresh thyme
- 1 tsp salt
- ½ tsp fresh ground black pepper
- 120ml/½ cup milk
- 120ml/½ cup double cream
- 1 tbsp fresh parsley, chopped

Method

1 Choose your preferred blend function, if required. Otherwise decide on your consistency at the end of cooking and then blend.

2 Cook the bacon in advance.

3 If your soup maker has a browning function, add the butter and onions first and leave to brown for a few minutes.

4 Meanwhile, cook the clams in a pan of water until they open – around 15 minutes. Remove the clams from their shells and roughly chop the meat.

5 Add all the ingredients, except the cream, bacon and parsley to the soup maker. Cover and leave to cook on high for 30 minutes. Ensure all the ingredients are well combined, tender and piping hot. Blend to your preferred consistency (or leave your machine to do this as programmed). Stir in the cream, crumbled bacon and parsley. Adjust the seasoning and serve.

CHEFS NOTE
Serve with oyster crackers.

SEAFOOD CHOWDER

Ingredients

- Knob of butter
- 1 medium onion, peeled and chopped
- 2 large potatoes, peeled and chopped
- 750ml/3 cups fish stock/broth
- 1 tsp salt

- 400g/14oz scallops, cooked
- 250ml/1 cup milk
- ½ tsp fresh ground black pepper
- 1 tbsp chopped fresh parsley
- 2 spring onions/scallions, chopped

Method

1 Choose your preferred blend function, if required. Otherwise decide on your consistency at the end of cooking and then blend.

2 Cook the scallops in advance.

3 If your soup maker has a browning function, add the butter, onions and potato first and leave to brown for a few minutes.

4 Add all the ingredients, except the parsley and spring onions, to the soup maker. Cover and leave to cook for 30 minutes. Ensure all the ingredients are well combined, tender and piping hot. Blend to your preferred consistency (or leave your machine to do this as programmed). Add the parsley and spring onions. Adjust the seasoning and serve.

CHEFS NOTE
Add a little cream for a richer soup.

i ♥ my soup maker

Soups Around The World

MINESTRONE

Ingredients

- 1 tbsp olive oil
- 1 small onion, peeled and chopped
- 500ml/2 cups tomato passata/sieved tomatoes
- 1 400g/14oz tin cannellini beans, rinsed and drained
- 60g/2½oz pasta

- 500ml/2 cups chicken stock/broth
- 1 tbsp oregano
- 1 small carrot, peeled and chopped
- 1 small parsnip, peeled and chopped
- Handful of cabbage, shredded
- 125g/4oz pancetta, cooked and finely chopped

Method

1 Choose your preferred blend function, if required. Otherwise decide on your consistency at the end of cooking and then blend.

2 Cook the pancetta in advance.

3 If your soup maker has a browning function, add the olive oil and onions first and leave to brown for a few minutes.

4 Add all the ingredients, except the cooked pancetta, to the soup maker. Cover and leave to cook on high for 30 minutes. Ensure all the ingredients are well combined, tender and piping hot. Blend to your preferred consistency (or leave your machine to do this as programmed). Add the pancetta, stir and leave to warm through for a further 2-3 minutes. Adjust the seasoning and serve.

CHEFS NOTE
If you don't have passata/sieved tomatoes, use a tin of chopped tomatoes instead.

MEDITERRANEAN VEGETABLE SOUP

Ingredients

- 1 tbsp olive oil
- 1 medium red onion, peeled and chopped
- 1lt/4 cups chicken or vegetable stock/broth
- 1 medium courgette/zucchini, chopped
- 1 medium red bell pepper, de-seeded and chopped
- 1 medium yellow bell pepper, de-seeded and chopped
- 1 tsp salt

Method

1 Choose your preferred blend function, if required. Otherwise decide on your consistency at the end of cooking and then blend. For this recipe, the chunky setting is recommended.

2 If your soup maker has a browning function, add the olive oil and onions first and leave to brown for a few minutes.

3 Add all the ingredients to the soup maker. Cover and leave to cook on high for 30 minutes. Ensure all the ingredients are well combined, tender and piping hot. Blend on the chunky setting (or leave your machine to do this as programmed). Adjust the seasoning and serve.

CHEFS NOTE
Feel free to vary the vegetables you use, and add herbs like oregano and basil for even more authentic Mediterranean flavour.

MULLIGATAWNY SOUP

Ingredients

- 1 tbsp olive oil
- 200g/7oz cooked lamb neck fillet, chopped or shredded
- 1 medium onion, peeled and chopped
- 1½ tbsp medium balti curry paste
- 1 medium carrot, peeled and chopped
- 1 medium parsnip, peeled and chopped
- 1 small potato, peeled and chopped

- 1 medium red bell pepper, de-seeded and chopped
- 500ml/2 cups passata/sieved tomatoes
- 500ml/2 cups chicken or vegetable stock/broth
- Salt and ground black pepper
- 125g/4oz basmati rice
- Fresh corriander/cilantro, to garnish

Method

1 Choose your preferred blend function, if required. Otherwise decide on your consistency at the end of cooking and then blend.

2 Cook the lamb in advance.

3 If your soup maker has a browning function add the olive oil and onions first and brown for a few minutes.

4 Stir the curry paste, lamb and onions together, then add all the other ingredients to the soup maker. Cover and leave to cook on high for 40 minutes. Ensure all the ingredients are well combined, tender and piping hot. Blend to your preferred consistency (or leave your machine to do this as programmed). Adjust the seasoning and serve garnished with fresh coriander.

CHEFS NOTE
A very tasty way to use up leftovers from your Sunday roast!

VICHYSSOISE

Ingredients

- 2 tbsp unsalted butter
- 2 medium leeks, chopped
- 1 medium onion, peeled and chopped
- 1 medium potato, peeled and chopped

- 750ml/3 cups chicken stock/broth
- Salt and pepper to taste
- 250ml/1 cup double cream

Method

1 Choose your preferred blend function, if required. For this recipe, it should be smooth. Otherwise decide on your consistency at the end of cooking and then blend.

2 If your soup maker has a browning function, add the butter, onions and leek first and leave to brown for a few minutes.

3 Add all the ingredients, except the cream, to the soup maker. Cover and leave to cook on high for 30 minutes. Ensure all the ingredients are well combined, tender and piping hot. Blend on the smooth setting (or leave your machine to do this as programmed). Adjust the seasoning, gently stir in the cream, and serve.

CHEFS NOTE
This soup is equally delicious chilled. Keep it in the fridge until you're ready to serve. Garnish with a dollop of soured cream and chopped chives.

MEXICAN CHILLI SOUP

Ingredients

- 1 tbsp olive oil
- 1 medium onion, peeled and chopped
- 1 red or green chilli, chopped
- 2 cloves garlic, peeled and crushed
- 250g/8oz cooked minced/ground beef
- 1 400g/14oz tin chopped tomatoes
- 1 400g/14oz tin red kidney beans, drained and rinsed

- 750ml/3 cups beef stock/broth
- 2 squares dark chocolate
- Salt and pepper
- 1 tbsp chopped fresh corriander/cilantro
- Dash of Tabasco sauce
- Soured cream to garnish
- Cheddar cheese, grated, to garnish

Method

1 Choose your preferred blend function, if required. Otherwise decide on your consistency at the end of cooking and then blend.

2 Cook the mince in advance.

3 If your soup maker has a browning function add the olive oil, onions, garlic and chilli first and leave to cook for a few minutes.

4 Add all the ingredients except the coriander, sour cream and Tabasco to the soup maker. Cover and leave to cook on high for 40 minutes. Ensure all the ingredients are well combined, tender and piping hot. Blend to your preferred consistency (or leave your machine to do this as programmed). Stir in the coriander and Tabasco. Adjust the seasoning and serve, garnished with soured cream and grated cheese.

CHEFS NOTE
Serve with plenty of nachos!

JAPANESE MISO SOUP

Ingredients

- 1lt/4 cups water
- 60ml/¼ cup warm water
- 3 tbsp miso
- 75g/3oz rice vermicelli
- 75g/3oz soft tofu, cubed

- 50g/2oz enoki mushrooms
- 3 spring onions/scallions, chopped
- Handful bean sprouts
- 2 tsp sesame seeds
- Few drops sesame oil

Method

1 Choose your preferred blend function, if required – chunky is recommended for this soup. Otherwise decide on your consistency at the end of cooking and then blend.

2 Dilute the miso in the warm water. Add all the ingredients, except the spring onions, bean sprouts, sesame seeds and oil, to the soup maker. Cover and leave to cook for 10 minutes, or until the vermicelli is cooked and all the ingredients are piping hot. Blend on the chunky setting. Stir in the spring onions, bean sprouts, sesame seeds and sesame oil, and serve.

CHEFS NOTE

Feel free to substitute any hard-to-obtain ingredients, e.g. use shiitake instead of enoki mushrooms.

CANJA DE GALINHA

Ingredients

- 1 tbsp olive oil
- 6 chicken thighs, cooked and chopped
- 1 medium onion, peeled and chopped
- 1lt/4 cups chicken stock/broth
- 2 medium carrots, peeled and chopped
- 2 medium potatoes, peeled and chopped
- 1 stalk celery, chopped
- 75g/3oz long grain rice
- 2 tbsp fresh parsley, chopped
- Salt and freshly ground black pepper

Method

1 Choose your preferred blend function, if required. Chunky is recommended for this recipe. Otherwise decide on your consistency at the end of cooking and then blend.

2 Cook the chicken in advance.

3 If your soup maker has a browning function add the olive oil and onions first and leave to cook for a few minutes.

4 Add all the ingredients, except the parsley, to the soup maker. Cover and leave to cook on high for 40 minutes. Ensure all the ingredients are well combined, tender and piping hot. Blend on the chunky setting (or leave your machine to do this as programmed)..

5 Adjust the seasoning and serve.

CHEFS NOTE

This simple, comforting soup is believed to help cure digestive complaints.

HUNGARIAN GOULASH SOUP

Ingredients

- 1 tbsp olive oil
- 2 medium onions, peeled and chopped
- 2 cloves garlic, peeled and crushed
- 1 red bell pepper, de-seeded and chopped
- 400g/14oz cooked spicy sausage, sliced
- 1 tbsp paprika

- 1 tsp caraway seeds
- 1 400g/14oz tin chopped tomatoes
- 1 tbsp tomato purée/paste
- Salt and freshly ground black pepper
- 750ml/3 cups beef stock/broth
- 1 large potato, peeled and chopped

Method

1 Choose your preferred blend function, if required – chunky is recommended for this recipe. Otherwise decide on your consistency at the end of cooking and then blend.

2 Cook the sausgaes in advance.

3 If your soup maker has a browning function add the olive oil, onions, garlic and pepper first and leave to cook for a few minutes.

4 Add all the ingredients to the soup maker. Cover and leave to cook on high for 40 minutes. Ensure all the ingredients are well combined, tender and piping hot. Blend on the chunky setting (or leave your machine to do this as programmed). Adjust the seasoning and serve.

CHEFS NOTE
Any type of cooked/cured spicy sausage or salami will work for this recipe.

BORSCHT

Ingredients

- 1 large beetroot, cooked, peeled and chopped
- 1 large potato, peeled and chopped
- 2 tbsp vegetable oil
- 1 medium onion, peeled and chopped
- 1 medium carrot, peeled and chopped
- ¼ head cabbage, chopped
- 1 400g/14oz tin kidney beans, drained and rinsed
- 750ml/3 cups chicken stock/broth
- 2 tbsp ketchup
- 2 tbsp lemon juice
- Salt and pepper

Method

1 Choose your preferred blend function, if required. Otherwise decide on your consistency at the end of cooking and then blend.

2 If your soup maker has a browning function, add the olive oil and onions first and leave to brown for a few minutes.

3 Add all the ingredients to the soup maker. Cover and leave to cook on high for 40 minutes. Ensure all the ingredients are well combined, tender and piping hot. Blend to your preferred consistency (or leave your machine to do this as programmed). Adjust the seasoning and serve.

CHEFS NOTE
Serve topped with a spoonful of soured cream.

ASIAN PORK SOUP

Ingredients

- 1 tbsp vegetable oil
- 350g/12oz cooked pork fillet, chopped
- 50g/2oz shiitake mushrooms
- 2 cloves garlic, peeled and crushed
- 750ml/3 cups chicken stock/broth
- 2 tbsp dry sherry

- 2 tbsp soy sauce
- 2 tsp fresh, grated ginger
- ¼ tsp crushed chilli flakes
- ½ Chinese Napa cabbage, shredded
- 1 spring onion/scallion, finely chopped

Method

1 Choose your preferred blend function, if required – chunky is recommended for this soup. Otherwise decide on your consistency at the end of cooking and then blend.

2 Cook the pork in advance.

3 Add all the ingredients, except the cabbage and spring onion, to the soup maker. Cover and leave to cook for 15 minutes. Ensure all the ingredients are well combined, tender and piping hot. Stir in the cabbage and spring onion and leave to warm through for a further 2-3 minutes. Blend on the chunky setting (or leave your machine to do this as programmed). Adjust the seasoning and serve.

CHEFS NOTE
Try also with pak choi instead of Napa cabbage.

 **CookNation**

Other COOKNATION TITLES

If you enjoyed 'I Love My Soup Maker' you may also be interested in other great cookbooks in the CookNation series.

You can browse all titles at www.bellmackenzie.com

Thank you.

Made in the USA
Middletown, DE
25 September 2019